Learn the alphabet Book

Copyright©. All rights reserved. No part of this book can be reproduced without Owners' Permission.

ISBN:978-1-916554-03-0

Hi! This is me Mia. I am on a journey to learn my ABC's. Come with me and learn as we go.

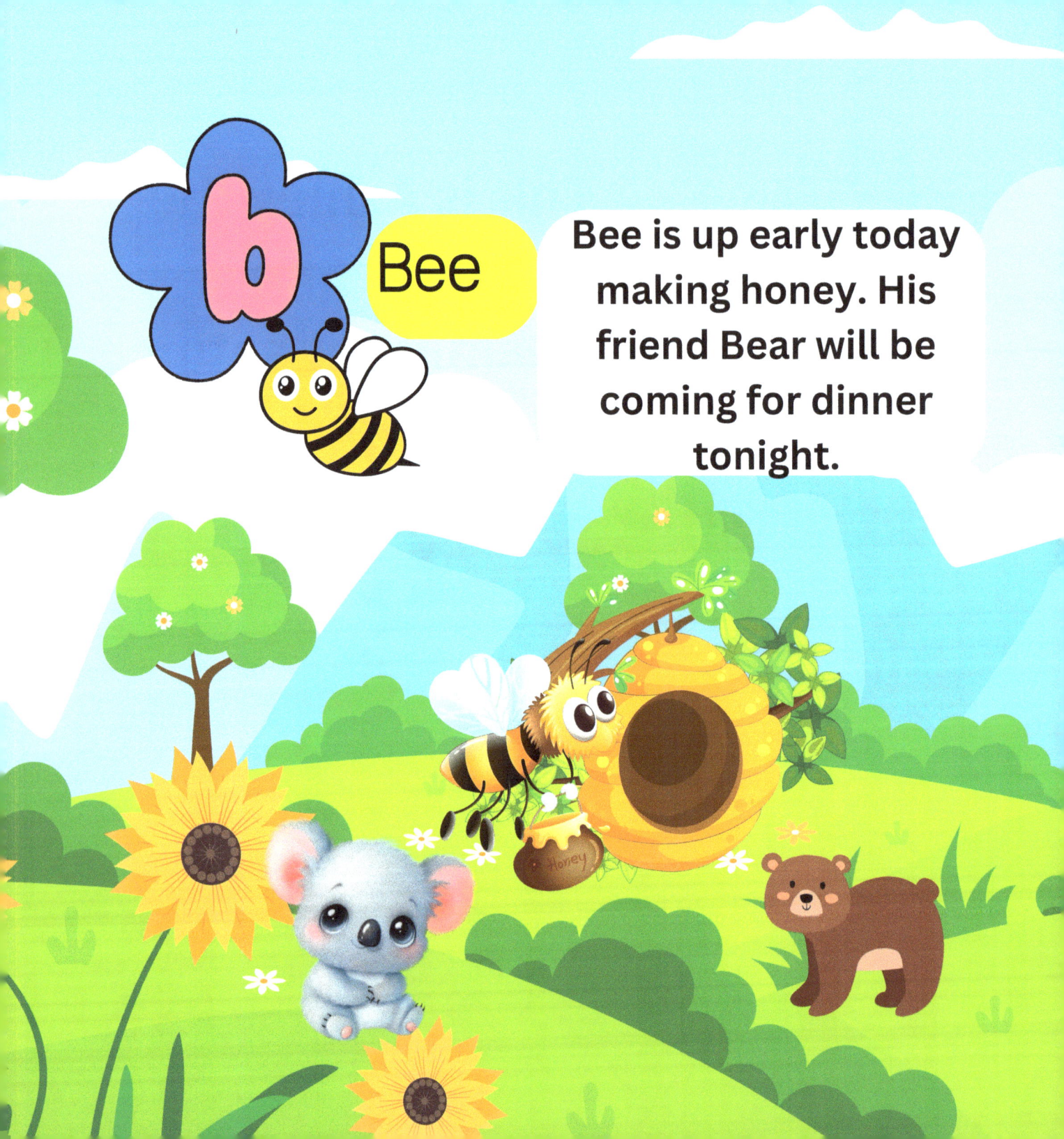

b Bee

Bee is up early today making honey. His friend Bear will be coming for dinner tonight.

frog

Fox has been up all night, so it's time to take a nap. Hi I'm Fred the frog , I can jump up and down all day with no trouble at all.

Baby giraffe is excited today. Her and mum has just received gifts from friends.

Giraffe

h
Hippo

Hippo is flying high today, thinking how does it feel like to live in a house?

igloo

Have you ever wondered if ice-cream would melt if kept inside an igloo?. "I am not sure said one of the impalas."

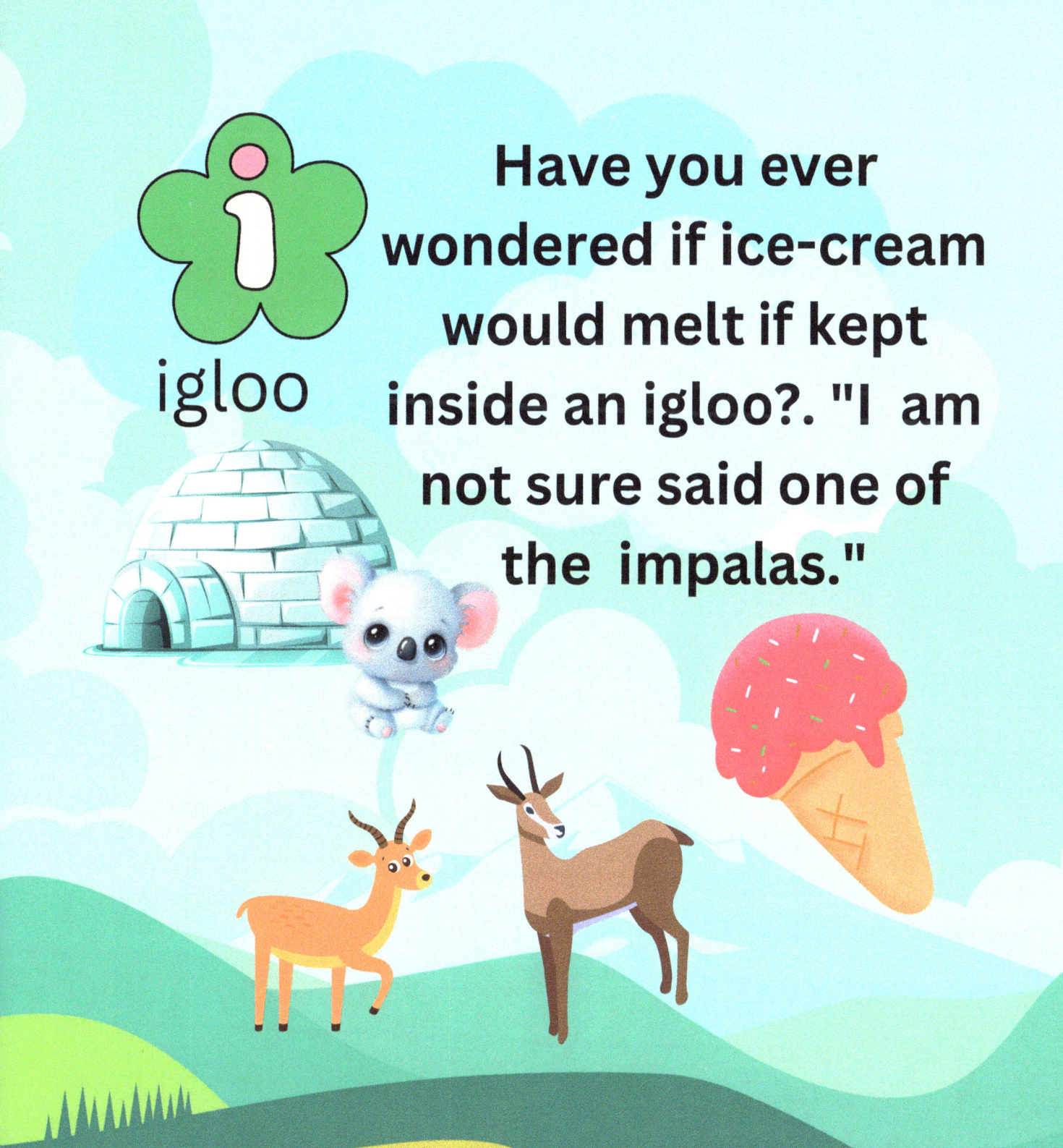

J

Jellyfish

Jellyfish was all excited to tell jaguar about all the adventure of his swimming in the sea.

K

kitten

Kitten really loved the music instrument kangaroo was playing. Do you know what it was?

l

Lion is the king of the jungle. I wonder what llama thinks about that.

Lion

Monkey

Monkey had a good day playing with the marbles.

Marbles

The newt loved watching the eggs in the nest every single day.

n

nest

O

The owl listened and watched carefully as the Beaver practised for the circus.

Owl

Penguin

Penguins love the the parachute, its the only way they can learn to fly.

R Rabbit

The rabbit enjoyed his carrot sitting next to the rocks.

q The quail grew new set of brightly colored feathers just as bright as the quilt.

quail

Happy Timmy the Tiger has stripes too many to count.

tiger

Turtle

unicorn

Is an umbrella useful for a unicorn?

Wolf

Wolf and whale needs a pack of new songs to sing.

The X-Ray Fish Will learn To play the xylophone for the singing competition.

xylophone

Zebra

At the zoo zebra had fun playing with all the children that came to visit.

www.ingramcontent.com/pod-product-compliance
Lightning Source LLC
Chambersburg PA
CBHW051322110526
44590CB00031B/4446